THE OLD SOUTH
Land of Many Dreams

Text by FRANK TAYLOR

Produced by
TED SMART and DAVID GIBBON

CRESCENT BOOKS
NEW YORK

CLB 1238
© 1985 Illustrations and text: Colour Library Books Ltd.,
   Guildford, Surrey, England.
Display and text filmsetting by Acesetters Ltd.,
   Richmond, Surrey, England.
Color separations by Llovet, S.A., Barcelona, Spain.
Printed and bound in Barcelona, Spain by Rieusset and Eurobinder.
All rights reserved.
Published 1985 by Crescent Books, distributed by Crown Publishers, Inc.
Printed and bound in Barcelona, Spain by Rieusset and Eurobinder.
ISBN 0 517 456222
h g f e d c b a

Describing, much less explaining, anything about the South, especially for a Southerner, is about as difficult as getting more than one cook to agree on what makes a good jambalaya. There are just too many distinctive ingredients. Actually, we Southerners are often accused of being mysterious about our makeup anyhow and are just as likely purposely to confuse anyone who shows too much interest in learning what makes us tick. Keeping outsiders guessing about what we'll do next, if anything, is our best defense.

To begin with, the South wasn't hospitable to outsiders. The only critters who seemed to be able to make a go of it were Indians, mosquitoes, alligators and a few Spanish friars, who could and would put up with anything. Hernando de Soto, a Spanish explorer, after wandering throughout the South in 1540-41 and finding irate Indians rather than gold, was about to say phooey when he got a fever – worse than the kind Southern women have always gotten when they needed to extricate themselves from a sticky social situation – died and was buried in the Mississippi River.

Ponce de León said "hasta luego" when he didn't find his fountain of eternal youth in 1513 – though millions of older folks still come to Florida thinking they're going to find it. And when he did come back to Florida in 1521, an Indian killed him on his first day ashore. Another Spaniard, Don Tristan de Luna, settled with his followers in Pensacola, Florida, but a hurricane finished them off two years later in 1561. Even the hardy English who landed on Roanoke Island off the North Carolina coast in 1585 (under the command of Sir Walter Raleigh) said, "thank you, no" and sailed back to England within a year. Their successors two years later simply disappeared and went down in history books as "The Lost Colony."

Finally, the Spanish managed to start a little settlement in St. Augustine, Florida in 1565, which is now the oldest city in the United States, and about 100 colonists founded the first permanent British settlement in Jamestown, Virginia in 1607.

Virginians started showing signs of being independent cusses early on, setting a pattern to be followed by the South as a whole in later years. By 1619 they had convinced London to give them a local government in the form of a House of Burgesses, the first representative legislature in America. It was Virginia-born Thomas Jefferson who, more than 150 years later, wrote the Declaration of Independence that made the 13 English colonies a new nation based on the principle that "All men are created equal."

Ironically, the Virginians, who defended so nobly their "inalienable rights... to life, liberty and the pursuit of happiness," were the recipients of the first cargo of African Negroes in 1619. Whereas white Europeans managed to reach these same shores by "indenturing" themselves as servants until they could pay the debt incurred in their passage, a legal system evolved that bound the Negroes to permanent slavery.

As predominant as slavery was, however, millions of Southerners did not own slaves. They were the pioneers who pushed back into the mountains and woods, hunting, fishing and wearing out the land before moving deeper into virgin territory. Fighting off Indians seemed no more tedious than fighting successive waves of British, French and Spanish invaders and bandits that harassed colonists in almost every early coastal settlement in the South. The pioneers were a rugged and self-reliant people, able to cope with harsh difficulties of survival. A gun and a hunting dog were man's best friend. Women simply had to make do, usually assuming a man's work with the growing of crops to feed the family. No fancy lace for them, notwithstanding the romantic notion of the Southern belle in hoop skirts. Life was rough and lonely. These people didn't have slaves, nor much sympathy for those who did.

The hill, or up-country folks actually resented what they perceived as the soft life of the low-country, or plantation types and the control they normally had over state politics, taxation, trade regulations and use of public funds. That contempt for planters was not as strong, however, as their hatred for any authority over their lives. So, when the North tried to force its will on the South in general, "country boys" with no personal interests in defending slavery were the bravest and meanest in fighting in alliance with planters against a common enemy from the North. And to this day if anyone from the "outside" suggests his way of doing anything is better than theirs, he might as well step on a hill of fire ants and stand still.

As rugged as life was in the back-country of the South, it was colorful and sociable. The names of festivals or events existing even today throughout the region suggest some of the carryings-on: rattlesnake roundups (seeing who can catch the most of them), rodeos, tobacco spitting contests, old-time fiddlers' conventions, bird dog trials, frog jumping contests, greased pig chases, wild turkey calling contests, hootenannies, hog rifle shoots and clog dances.

Unlike in the North, where education was cared for by the church and local governments at an early date, in the South teaching was for many generations left to the family. In the predominantly rural areas a child did not usually advance beyond the rudimentary skill level of his parents in reading, writing and 'rithmetic.

In contrast, the wealthy planters hired private tutors to give their children an essentially classical education, then sent their offspring to Europe for university studies. The College of William and Mary, created in 1693 in Williamsburg, Virginia, provided the first chance to get a proper higher education in the colonies. This limited education system helped reinforce a social hierarchy topped by a planter aristocracy which, from Virginia alone, supplied four of the nation's first five presidents.

Planters, and the bankers and traders who got rich with them, also spent money grandly in building some of the world's most beautiful homes. Charleston, South Carolina, founded in 1670, grew to be one of the busiest and most prosperous ports of trade with Europe. It also became an architectural landmark, making it one of the "must" places to visit on a tour of the Old South.

No expense was spared in equipping these homes with the finest of European furniture. Entertaining was lavish. Dress was regal. Manners were courtly. The art of conversation hung thicker than family portraits in parlors. Slaves vied for a position on the manor staff as some of the civility there was extended to them, and saved them from the brute hands of field bosses.

But all of that glitter and glamour was made possible by a social system that had four million people in bondage by 1861. Of course, some owners treated their slaves humanely. Most entrusted their children's upbringing to a Negro mammy so that strong sentimental bonds developed between white and black. But relatively few slaves were ever given the chance to obtain education or any other means to acquire their freedom, even in those cases where the law might permit such a transaction.

Not only did the system break the hearts and minds of those it enslaved, but it also split the soul of the new nation. Abolitionists in the North began publicly attacking slavery in the 1820s and 1830s. Southerners, who until then had defended slavery on an economic basis, began arguing about racial superiority to explain why the Negro was "fit" for his role as servant. That perverse argument, fanatically believed, persisted long after many a white column collapsed in front of most manor houses.

Southerners were already on the defensive because, during the years 1775 to 1830, the North was industrializing and gaining economic superiority over the South. Southerners became a minority on the political and economic scenes. In self-defense they became ardent proponents of states' rights.

Trouble between the North and the South developed over the balance between states that permitted slavery and those that did not. The scorecard was important because each state had two seats in the all-powerful United States Senate. A bitter controversy was solved by allowing Missouri to enter the Union in 1819 as a slave state, and Maine in 1820 as a free state. But then in 1824 Southerners resented John Quincy Adams, a

Yankee, winning the presidential election over their candidate, Andrew Jackson. When Adams pushed for high protective tariffs in 1828, Southerners attacked the measure, saying it would harm them and only benefit manufacturers in the North. When tariffs were increased still further in 1832, South Carolina's John C. Calhoun, then Vice President of the country, argued that each state had the right to nullify a federal law it felt was unconstitutional, and his state did just that with the tariff law. By that time South Carolina was already threatening to secede from the Union, a threat not carried out because the federal government backed down on the tariff issue.

But tension grew over the admission of new states after the U.S. won vast new territories, including Texas, from Mexico in 1848 and then created the new territories of Kansas and Nebraska in 1854.

Compromises seemed to keep the fragile nation together at the last minute, but the explosiveness of the situation increased. Criticism of the South's slavery policy further inflamed relations between the two regions. Harriet Beecher Stowe's novel *Uncle Tom's Cabin*, published in 1852, infuriated the South with its portrait of the horrors of slavery. In 1859 John Brown, an abolitionist, tried to incite a general slave uprising by attacking the federal arsenal at Harpers Ferry, Virginia (now in West Virginia). He was captured and hanged, but hanged also were the hopes of a tranquil solution to the slavery question.

The last straw was the election to the presidency of Abraham Lincoln, an opponent of slavery, in 1860. South Carolina seceded from the Union on December 20th. By January, Alabama, Florida, Georgia, Louisiana and Mississippi followed suit and formed the Confederate States of America. They appointed Jefferson Davis as president, designed a rebel flag (still seen widely today when more than one Southerner is gathered for whatever purpose), and made Montgomery, Alabama (later Richmond, Virginia) their capital. In 1861 Arkansas, North Carolina, Tennessee, Texas and Virginia joined the Confederacy. Southerners still refer to the conflict as the "War Between the States" and Yankees call it "The War of the Rebellion," a difference which shows the irreconcilability of the two sides regarding the very nature of the war and its causes. The Civil War began on April 12, 1861 when Southern forces opened fire on the U.S. Army posts at Fort Sumter at Charleston, South Carolina.

The Confederate Army under General Stonewall Jackson gained an upper hand at first by routing federal troops at the First Battle of Manassas (or Bull Run as it is also called). But the North, with superior financial and industrial strength and a larger army, finally took the edge. General Robert E. Lee and his Southern forces were thrown back decisively at Antietam (Maryland) in September, 1862 and at Gettysburg, Pennsylvania in mid-1863.

By that time President Lincoln had issued the "Emancipation Proclamation" (on January 1, 1863) freeing all slaves. With the victory of Union troops at Gettysburg he made his famous "Gettysburg Address" in which he called for "a new birth of freedom" with a "government of the people, by the people, for the people..."

The embittered South fought on, even after General Ulysses S. Grant took Vicksburg, Mississippi in July, 1863, thus gaining control over the entire length of the Mississippi River and isolating Arkansas, Louisiana and Texas which had provided essential supply routes into the South.

In 1864 General William Tecumseh Sherman (don't mention his name in Georgia), made his infamous march to the sea from Chattanooga, Tennessee, to Savannah, Georgia, burning everything in his path, including Atlanta; it was this destruction that Margaret Mitchell depicted dramatically in her book *Gone with the Wind*.

Finally, Confederate resistance wore down. On April 9, 1865, the commander of the Southern forces, General Robert E. Lee, surrendered to General Grant at the Appomattox Court House in Virginia.

The South fell under military occupation and was forced to comply with federal laws in order to be readmitted to the Union. Northern politicians, businessmen and a hearty collection of scoundrels came to the South so fast as profiteers that they couldn't have had time to pack more than a small "carpetbag" or suitcase and thus became known and despised as "carpetbaggers." Southerners who conspired with them were called "scalawags" or just plain varmints.

And then there were new laws. Congress passed the thirteenth amendment to the Constitution in 1865 outlawing slavery throughout the United States, the fourteenth amendment in 1868 giving citizenship to blacks and the fifteenth in 1870 making it illegal to deprive anyone of the right to vote on the basis of race.

By massive registration and voting of blacks, the Republican Party, which had its strength in the North, was able to dominate Southern politics for several years. Blacks had their representatives in a number of state legislatures and controlled the government in South Carolina with a majority. The sudden change enraged whites. The Ku Klux Klan was founded in Tennessee soon after the war's end, and membership spread like wildfire throughout the South. They emblazoned many a Southern night with their white, pointed hoods and their torches as they rode across country burning enormous crosses and terrorizing the Negro population and anyone who dared sympathize with blacks. As sunrise lit the dawns many a dead Negro was found dangling from rope tied to the twisted branch of an oak tree. The campaign of terror effectively kept black men out of politics and shut the mouths of white sympathizers.

The Ku Klux Klan disappeared as the whites' need for it diminished with their growing power. However, the organization was revived about 1915 in Atlanta and struck out not only against Negroes, but also immigrants, Jews and especially Roman Catholics. The organization has ebbed and flowed since, but in some Southern towns today one can still call the KKK hot line to hear "news" of who's doing what wrong, according to them, if not a suggestion for the need of some vigilante justice.

That reoccurrence of activities, the attachment to certain traditions, the determination of most Southerners to continue to separate themselves from the rest of the nation with whatever behavior sets them apart, suggests the difficulty in arbitrarily dividing old South from new.

Sure, the South has come a long way in modernizing and in treating all of its people more fairly and decently. Now it's called the "Sun Belt" rather than the "Cotton Belt." And it's even "putting on the dogs", becoming so swanky that they got a Georgia peanut farmer elected president of the nation in 1976, the bi-centennial year of independence.

TEXAS

Southerners have always talked about themselves and

said, "And then there's Texas." Texans only talk and think about Texas. How did Texas get so big for its boots? Well, it is BIG, bigger than any other state in the nation except Alaska. And Texans have always been bold.

That's how they got started, by declaring themselves independent of Mexico in 1836. The Mexicans had never done much with Texas, like their Spanish forebears who first went there in 1519 and subsequently established a few missions. Mexico even invited American colonists into Texas in the early 1820s, a door it tried unsuccessfully to close in 1830. In 1836 Mexican dictator Antonio Lopez de Santa Ana led troops to put the "Yankees" in their place.

In the most famous stand of white men in the West, the Mexicans killed the legendary band of 187 defenders of the Alamo, a small mission in San Antonio. Dead were heroes like Davy Crockett, Jim Bowie and William Barrett Travis. Santa Ana learned that Texans are like hornets. You don't mess with their nest. With the cry "Remember the Alamo," Texan troops under Sam Houston routed the Mexicans in a victory that gave birth to Texan pride. The new republic became a state in 1845.

As many early settlers came from other Southern states, Texas joined the Confederacy and funneled critical supplies from Mexico to its army until the Union Army took Vicksburg in 1863 and gained control of the Mississippi River. The last battle of that war was fought at Palmito Hill, Texas, near the mouth of the Rio Grande on May 13, 1865, as the news of Lee's surrender a month earlier hadn't reached the two armies in Texas.

Reconstruction was harsher on Texas than the war itself had been, thus breeding further scepticism toward outsiders. Cotton planters had done well in north and central Texas before the war. But during Reconstruction it was the ranchers who opened the state, pushing into the vast, western, lone prairies against the over-whelming opposition of fierce winters and fiercer Indians. It was an epic saga of hardship, bloodshed and suffering, the stuff that brought out the "baddest of the bad" in outlaws like Jesse James and gave Hollywood material a century later for a generation of cowboy movies. In that environment a man, woman or child had to be self-sufficient; a trait ever present in the soul of a Texan.

Visitors wanting to capture the Old South today in

Texas must see the Alamo, the Spanish Governor's Palace and "La Villita" (the restored 19th century town) of San Antonio, the Varner-Hogg Plantation, built in 1835, where the First Congress of the Republic of Texas took place in 1836 in West Columbia, and the Frontier Fair at the site of Fort Richardson in Jacksboro, used by the cavalry to save white scalps from the marauding Indians of the area. Once the Indian threat had receded in the 1880s Victorian houses started lining the streets of towns like Gainesville where Texans could finally put a little charm into their Southern living.

But the best way to get a feel for the Old South here is to wander the great expanse of striking and often stark landscapes and meet Texans their own ground. In spite of the enormous economic transition after the discovery of oil in 1901, the nature of Texans was never diluted. They are what they are and always have been. And they still believe that everything is biggest and best in Texas.

ARKANSAS

Look for puffs of smoke snaking out of the chimneys of rustic log cabins nestled in piney woods along winding rivers teeming with catfish. Listen to the farmer chide his mule to draw his plow through soil that moans "not again" to start another arduous cycle on the land. This way you'll get to know the languorous and strenuous life in Arkansas on the western frontier of the Old South.

After Hernando de Soto's trip into Arkansas in 1541 no one else bothered to pay their respects for at least another 100 years, until a Jesuit priest, Jacques Marquette, and a French trader, Louis Jolliet, came exploring. Their visit was followed in 1686 by a French settlement of a trading post called Arkansas Post, the first permanent white settlement west of the Mississippi River, which later became the first capital of the territory. As increasing numbers of settlers came to, or more often passed through Arkansas, the original inhabitants (the Cherokee, Osage, Comanche and Shoshone Indians) resented the trespassing on their lands and used a lot of war paint and arrows trying to dissuade it.

So when planters in the southeastern states were building manors outwardly displaying their wealth, Arkansas frontiersmen as late as the early 19th century were building inwardly with forts like the one at Fort

Smith. The frontier experience and spirit so captivated the imagination of city slickers back East that authors like Washington Irving came to Fort Smith, as he did in 1836, to write about the westward-ho movement.

Many early residents planted cotton in Arkansas, and some of them got rich. The stately Bonneville House in Fort Smith is a reminder of the genteel life-style the first prominent families created in such contrast to the rickety, earth-floored slave quarters in back of their glamorous homes, the boisterous saloons where arguments were often settled with bullets, and the "bawdy" houses where pleasure could be purchased for the right price.

Many people left Arkansas, like the 5,000 in 1849 who packed their bare belongings and rich dreams into wagon trains leaving Fort Smith for the California gold fields. But those who stayed set to building a permanent home. They moved the territorial capital to Little Rock and as early as 1819 hewed oak logs by hand, covered them with cypress siding and inaugurated their first capitol building. That structure was remodeled in 1834, two years before Arkansas became a state, and can be seen today.

Arkansas seceded from the Union and fought bravely, although totally unprepared, for the Confederacy. One of its most fabled battles, now referred to as the "forgotten battle," took place at Prairie Grove in the Ozark Mountains. There frontiersmen with their squirrel rifles stubbornly held off Union soldiers and cavalrymen throughout the day. At night they padded their wagon wheels and horses' hooves with quilts and blankets and slipped unheard down the western flank of the Ozarks into the town of Van Buren, where they celebrated their smart-aleckness with chortles and hearty swigs of corn whiskey. It's times and tales like that that have lessened the sting of humiliation and defeat in the minds of every Southerner.

LOUISIANA

Just as America's greatest river, the Mississippi, brought a wealth of soil and deposits to the Louisiana delta at its mouth on the Gulf of Mexico, so too did it attract a rich variety of peoples and cultural influences to the "Bayou State." A Frenchman, René-Robert Vavelier, Sieur de La Salle, first claimed the area for France in 1682 and named it for King Louis XIV. Pierre Le Moyne, Sieur d'Iberville, started a colony in 1699, and his brother, Jean Baptiste Le Moyne, Sieur de Bienville, founded New Orleans in 1718 and named it for Philippe, Duc d'Orléans. A Spanish governor ruled over the area from 1762 to 1796, aiding the 13 colonies in their Revolutionary War against England, then relinquishing power again to the French who eventually sold the Louisiana Territory to the United States (a purchase that included land northward to the Canadian border) in 1803. In 1812 Louisiana became a state. During the War of 1812 the English invaded but were eventually thrown out by Andrew Jackson and a rag-tag band of backwoodsmen in the battle of Chalmette near New Orleans. Soldiers again filled the streets of New Orleans in the 1830s on their way to fight the Mexicans in Texas. In 1862 troops came the other way into the city as Admiral David G. Farragut of the Union Navy invaded this key Confederate port.

Taking New Orleans was an important symbolic victory for the Union forces as one Louisianan, General Pierre Gustave Toutant Beauregard, was the man who fired the first shot on Fort Sumter that started the Civil War and another, Judah P. Benjamin, was the Secretary of War then Secretary of State of the Confederacy under its President Jefferson Davis.

Yankees in New Orleans had their hands full trying to understand what any of the locals were saying. Southerners were bad enough, but French was still an official language of the area until after the Civil War. And then there were the descendants of the Acadians from Nova Scotia who had intermarried with the Negro slaves and Indians and spoke "Cajun", which they still do their best to keep anyone from understanding except themselves.

Long before the war sugarcane made many people rich in Louisiana, especially after the invention in 1795 of a process to granulate sugar from cane juice. Slaves became the backbone of the sugar and later rice plantation economy. But the Negroes also made a major cultural contribution, starting with their drumbeating and tribal dancing on Congo Square (now Beauregard Square) and later with a hot, syncopated music called jazz. They gave New Orleans an exotic allure still present today in its French Quarter.

Early morning sounds and smells in the Quarter evoke olden days, with ample-bodied vendors in straw hats hawking mangos, bananas and string beans at the French Market along the river, and locals grudgingly beginning a new day at a nearby cafe, sipping chicory coffee and nibbling at a French beignet (doughnut) or a piece of Cajun "pain-perdu" (a type of French bread). A stroll down the narrow streets of the French Quarter, and a peek through elaborately designed wrought iron fences dripping with cascades of wisteria and bougainvillea, reveal the internal courtyards and rows of slaves' quarters behind the townhouses many plantation owners built to permit them to satiate their every whim and fancy in the rowdy city, and to offset the relative peacefulness of country life. The garden district of New Orleans, with its Greek Revival houses, is a showcase matched only by Charleston, South Carolina, in its grandeur and beauty.

As exciting as New Orleans is, the rest of the state must be seen. In fact, when moviemakers wanted to picture the South as it used to be they went to Clinton to film *The Long Hot Summer* and *The Sound and the Fury* and to Houmas House in Burnside to film *Hush, Hush Sweet Charlotte*. Oak Alley, a Greek Revival mansion in Vacherie, built in the 1830s, with branches of two parallel rows of old oaks forming a canopy from the house to the Mississsippi River, is still one of the most photographed homes in America. Oakley, in St. Francisville is the home in which John James Audubon worked as a tutor to the plantation children, while sketching many of the birds he included in his fabulous book *Birds of America*.

To protect all this heritage, Louisianans weren't above sly trickery in the Civil War. When a Yankee attack was imminent in the vicinity of Fort Humbug, which wasn't properly armed, local troops blackened hollowed out logs and put them in place to look like cannons. Thankfully, the approaching invaders veered off course and didn't call the bluff.

ALABAMA

Alabama means "thicket clearers" in the Choctaw Indian language, and that's what early settlers spent most of their time doing.

Getting Indians out of the thickets wasn't easy. One of the bloodiest and most ruthless battles with Indians in American history took place in Alabama in 1540, when Hernando de Soto fought and killed thousands of Choctaw warriors under Chief Tuscaloosa, at Mabila. De Soto came and left, but the Indians stayed put, resisting any other intrusion into their lands.

Finally, in 1702, a small band of French Canadians under Pierre Le Moyne, Sieur d'Iberville, built Fort Louis on the Mobile River. Nine years later that first settlement was transferred to Fort Conde, the present site of the city of Mobile, and became the capital of the French colonial empire in America until 1722, when New Orleans assumed the role.

Alabama's Indians must have been confused as to who their enemy was as "ownership" of the area changed several times over the next century. The Treaty of Paris in 1763, ending the French and Indian War, gave England control of the Mobile area. The Spanish in Florida ruled from 1783 to 1813, when the U.S. flag went up the pole at Mobile. That same year the Creek Indians attacked Fort Mims in force and massacred several hundred whites. Because of that loss, renowned Indian fighter Andrew Jackson (whose nickname was "Old Hickory") came after the Creeks with a vengeance and defeated them soundly at Horseshoe Bend in March, 1814, the site of which battle is now a national park.

Cotton became king early in Alabama, and Montgomery became capital of the kingdom. On February 18, 1861 Jefferson Davis, a cotton planter in Mississippi and former U.S. Secretary of War under President Franklin Pierce, was sworn in on the steps of Alabama's capitol as the President of the Confederate States of America. Montgomery still proudly refers to itself as the "Cradle of the Confederacy." The capital of the Confederacy, however, was transferred to Richmond, Virginia in May, 1861, shortly after that state seceded from the Union.

Alabama lived up to its state motto: "We Dare Defend Our Rights." But like the rest of the South it fell before the onslaught of Northern forces. A famous naval battle took place in Mobile Bay in 1864 when Admiral David G. Farragut stormed Ft. Morgan and blockaded Mobile, one of the principal ports of the Confederacy. Luckily, most of Alabama escaped the devastation suffered by its neighbor, Georgia.

Although most Alabamans, black and white, remained very poor well into the 20th century, the state did take a lead in offering educational opportunities to blacks by opening, in 1881, the Tuskegee Institute under the leadership of Booker T. Washington.

About that time the state was also jumping into the industrial age in Birmingham by firing its first blast furnace to make steel.

But Alabama, with its giant, moss-draped oak trees standing tall, like sentinels guarding the past, still looks much as it did in the old days. The waterfall in Selma has been called the greatest antebellum riverfront in existence in America. And the 35-mile long Azalea Trail through Mobile winds past white-columned homes where history still sits rocking on the porch. Oakleigh, built in the 1830s as a retreat into elegance, seems as far removed from the first thicket clearings as it does from today.

MISSISSIPPI

Mississippi, the "Magnolia State," can be as difficult to spell as it is to understand. Poor by socio-economic standards, it has long been one of the richest states in folklore and literary genius.

If you eat "mud pie" (made of chocolate, not dirt), attend the tobacco-spitting championship of the world or read William Faulkner, you're talking about Mississippi. It was at Sunflower Landing, Mississippi that Hernando de Soto first caught sight of the mighty Mississippi River in 1540. He died before his expedition returned eastward, and he was buried in the river. La Salle claimed the area for France in 1680 and Pierre Le Moyne, Sieur d'Iberville made the first settlement in 1699 near the present site of Biloxi.

The jewel of Mississippi is Natchez, named for the Indians who massacred the first French settlers in 1729. The French, aided by the Choctaw Indians, recovered the area only to lose it later to the Spaniards. It was here that, in 1797, the American flag was raised for the first time in the lower Mississippi River Valley. From the time the first steamboat landed at Natchez in 1811, the town prospered. Natchez-under-the-Hill, the lower part of the town on the river, was a hotbed of sex, gambling and killing. The upper part of the town was genteel. Remnants of its elegant past may be viewed in the annual spring "Pilgrimage" when sweet-talking, hoop-skirted ladies guide visitors through about 30 magnificent homes in the area. One of these homes, the "Briars" is the plantation home where Jefferson Davis' wife, Varina Howell, grew up.

Many a settler came to Mississippi across the "Natchez Trace," originally a crude path used by Indians and wild animals extending from Nashville, Tennessee and abounding in snakes, robbers and Indians. It was the route Andrew Jackson took on his way to meet the

British at the Battle of New Orleans during the War of 1812. Plantation owners from the Carolinas and Virginia came to Mississippi on the Trace seeking the state's rich soils for their cotton crops. William Randolph of Virginia founded the town of Holly Springs, where many planters built magnificent mansions.

Nearby Oxford grew up as the home of the University of Mississippi ("Ole Miss") and later of William Faulkner, who referred to the town as "Jefferson" in several of his novels. St. Peter's Cemetery is now the permanent home of Lucius Quintus Cincinnatus Lamar – a good Southern name – who drafted the Order of Secession making Mississippi the second state to secede from the Union. After the war he became a Supreme Court Justice and worked to bring the two regions together peacefully.

July 4, 1863 is a date Mississippians will not forget or forgive. That's the day that General Ulysses S. Grant, after a 47-day siege, captured Vicksburg, the "Gibraltar of the Confederacy." That battle and the simultaneous one at Gettysburg sealed the fate of the South. In control of Vicksburg, Union forces could cut off supplies to the Confederate troops coming across the Mississippi from the West. Not until the 1940s would the citizens of Vicksburg celebrate the national independence date of July 4, so embittered were they by that defeat on the same date. They're still getting even by digging up old Yankee cannon balls from trenches that pockmark the state, and selling them back to Northern tourists as souvenirs, at a high price, mind you.

Nothing much changed in Mississippi because of the war. They still salute the Confederate flag and sing Dixie, the South's national anthem. They still move slowly. And most of the people in the rural areas are still dirt poor. And all of them talk with a drawl thicker and slower than molasses.

FLORIDA

With no youth-preserving waters, no gold and a heap of mean Indians, Florida wasn't fit for human habitation. So thought the Spaniards until some French Hugenot Protestants decided to live on the St. Johns River in 1564. So it was that Don Pedro Menendez de Anilos founded St. Augustine on September 8, 1565. He wiped out the French, and his town became the first permanent white settlement in America. After 1763 the English took over Florida, but traces of the original Spanish influence survive today.

Florida became so devoted to the British Crown that John Hancock and John Adams, signers of the Declaration of Independence, were hung in effigy in St. Augustine. The unappreciative English gave Florida back to Spain in 1783. Finally, in 1813, Spain sold Florida to the United States for $5 million. Indian fighter Andrew Jackson became the first governor. But a series of wars with Seminole Indians up through the late 1850s kept Florida in turmoil. Except for a few Indians who managed to seek refuge in the Everglades, most of Florida's Indians were deported to the West. Tropical diseases like malaria, yellow fever and cholera also took their toll on the early settlers.

Floridians meant business when they put their motto on their state flag: "Let Us Alone." So when South Carolina seceded from the Union, Florida wasn't far behind in seeking its own self-rule. Union troops struck early in Florida and controlled most of its forts and ports. Florida had as many as 60,000 slaves working the cotton and tobacco plantations of its northern region, but it quickly became a haven for runaway or freed slaves seeking a new home.

But the big influx of new residents came after the war, with Northerners flocking to the Florida sunshine. The state's population grew from 140,000 in 1860 to 270,000 in 1880. Drainage projects in South Florida made land suitable for settlement and farming. Cubans started rolling cigars in Tampa's Ybor City in the 1880s and a Chinese named Lue Gim Gong started planting orange groves on the East Coast.

Then came the railroads and opulent hotels. Henry Plant linked Richmond, Virginia and Tampa, Florida with the Atlantic Coastline Railroad and built the luxurious Tampa Bay Hotel, festooned with minarets, to lure tourists southward. Henry Morrison Flagler took his East Coast Railroad passengers further south from St. Augustine, where he built the Ponce de León Hotel to a place just north of Daytona Beach, where he erected the fancy Ormond Hotel. Later he put rails down to a sandy dead end of the line that he called Palm Beach and built the Breakers Hotel with enough poshness to attract the likes of the Rockefellers and Vanderbilts. In 1896 he extended the line to Biscayne Bay and started the village of Miami.

In spite of all the razzle-dazzle development that often led to architectural exuberance of dubious taste, Floridians still treasure the quiet charm and elegance of St. Augustine, which boasts of having the oldest Spanish house, the oldest schoolhouse, the oldest store and even the oldest alligator farm in America. It's a wonder the city survived at all with so many attempts to burn, sack, storm or cannonball it, starting in 1586 when Sir Francis Drake's men set it on fire.

Equally persevering at the far Western end of the state, in its "panhandle," is Pensacola, said to have changed hands 17 times and lived under five flags. Successive waves of Spaniards had more luck than Don Tristan de Luna, whose settlement of 1559 was destroyed by a storm in 1561, a fate many more modern residents have also had to cope with. They left their Hispanic mark on what was to become a strategic lumber and shipping center.

Between those two northern cities lies the Suwannee River, meandering from Georgia to the Gulf of Mexico underneath boughs of cypress trees draped melancholically with Spanish moss. Stephen Foster immortalized that beautiful river in a song that still fills the heart of Southerners away from home with a nostalgic longing to be back where they feel they belong.

GEORGIA

The state associated with peaches, buzzards, crackers and goobers first belonged to the Creek and Cherokee Indians. Hernando de Soto tromped through it in 1540 looking for gold. Had he looked in Dahlonega he might have found nuggets like the ones that led to America's first gold rush there in 1828. By 1566 a few Spanish missions were in place along the Atlantic coast. Not until February, 1773, near the present site of Savannah, did the English settlement under the command of General James Edward Oglethorpe take root. He brought a motley crew of debtors and misfits – to the kind of exile the English called humanitarian, you know, give the boys a second chance, someplace else, far away. The colony, the last of the original 13 in America, was more important as a buffer against the Spanish to the south in Florida. The colony, named for King George II, attracted many other north European immigrants who started planting rice and cotton. Eli Whitney invented his cotton gin near Savannah in 1793, and cotton became a major export crop.

Savannah, which followed a plan designed by Oglethorpe, became a bustling port. The first steamship to cross the Atlantic Ocean (the S.S. Savannah) made its maiden voyage in 1819 in 29 days from Savannah to Liverpool.

Traders and bankers built substantial Regency and Georgian houses, many of which stand today along with the Green-Meldrim House, birthplace of Juliette Gordon Low, founder of the Girl Scouts movement. John and Charles Wesley, founders of Methodism, preached their religion to early settlers at Christ Church in nearby St. Simons Island.

As the colonists pushed further inland they came up against the Cherokee Indians who had, at a place near Echota, Georgia, the capital of their nation from 1825-38. At that time a treaty banned the Cherokees from Georgia, an act the United States Supreme Court declared unconstitutional. But old Indian fighter Andrew Jackson, then president, defied that ruling and drove the Cherokees out to Oklahoma on the infamous "Trail of Tears."

White Georgians shed their own tears when General Sherman burned Atlanta to the ground in the fall of 1864. The Battle of Atlanta is dramatically depicted in a three-dimensional panoramic painting in the "Cyclorama" in Atlanta's Grant Park, a major tourist attraction. Confederate heroes Jefferson Davis, Robert E. Lee and Stonewall Jackson appear in massive (140-foot-high) carvings near Atlanta on the face of Stone Mountain, the world's largest chunk of exposed granite.

From Atlanta Sherman continued his pestilential march to the sea at Savannah, destroying railroads, bridges, factories, mills, public buildings, plantations, farms – everything – in a 60-mile-wide path. Sherman wired President Abraham Lincoln from Savannah offering him the city as a Christmas present.

In spite of all the hatred, destruction and mistrust on both sides and what looked like the end of the world in Margaret Mitchell's book and the film *Gone with the Wind*, the famous line of one of the characters, Scarlett O'Hara, was prophetic: "Tomorrow is another day."

That new day dawned early in Atlanta. The capital was moved there from Milledgeville in 1868. Atlanta was a young city, founded only in 1837 and first named "Terminus" because it was the end of the Western-Atlantic Railroad. But it quickly healed its wounds, started rebuilding and soon became the commercial and transportation center of the South.

Luckily not all of Georgia was destroyed during the war. The town of Washington (where the movie *Tobacco Road* was filmed), for instance, has some 40 antebellum homes dating as far back as 1790. Other towns with an Old South flavor include Madison, Athens and Thomasville.

Whether old or new, Georgia, like all the South, is a state of mind for those born to it, one that evokes a feeling of nostalgia, like an "old sweet song" as Hoagy Carmichael wrote in the words to his song "Georgia on my Mind" – now the state's official song – "...clear as moonlight through the pines."

TENNESSEE

Tennesseans, in spite of having mountain barriers pinning them in, had a hard time staying put. They were always marching off to someone else's battle, which is a good reason for Tennessee being called the Volunteer State.

Davy Crockett, born in Limestone, Tennessee in 1786, went to Texas, as did teacher Sam Houston and David Bowie, to help Texans win their independence from Mexico. And Andrew Jackson spent years driving Indians out of the South, and the British out of New Orleans in the War of 1812.

The state derives its name from "Tenassee," the capital of the Cherokee Indians, and was a part of North Carolina until 1785. A few years earlier Daniel Boone had carved the "Wilderness Road" through the Cumberland Gap, permitting waves of westward migration that were eventually to travel far beyond Tennessee's western border.

The state's first town was Jonesboro, still one of its most picturesque, founded in 1779. Pioneers built Fort Nashborough a year later in what is now Nashville on the Cumberland River. The reconstructed fort gives a good idea of how the early frontiersmen lived and protected themselves against Indians. This rustic building is in utter contrast to the Greek Revival State Capitol, completed in Nashville in 1855 in a style that became so widely used in a region of such overall roughness and poverty. The Belle Meade mansion nearby, known as the "Queen of Tennessee

Plantations," is a good example of that radical transition from log cabin to manor house. Another showplace of civilized architecture in the area is "The Hermitage," the beautiful house of Andrew Jackson, who later became president of the United States.

Not everyone in Tennessee agreed with the manor style of life nor the economic system that supported it. The Cumberland and Smoky Mountains divided the state both geographically and in the way people thought. The flatlands to the West of the mountains were a perfect setting for large, slave-holding cotton plantations which made that region want to unite with the cause of the Confederacy. Front Street in Memphis, on the Mississippi River, became one of the busiest cotton markets in the world. East Tennessee, an area of small farms, tried to prevent the state's secession from the Union. In fact, Tennessee was the last state of the eleven to join the "rebellion," and many of its residents, especially from the eastern part, joined Union troops in the fighting.

Chattanooga, where Cherokee Indians started their forced marches westward to exile in the 1830s, was the site of strategic Civil War battles. Sherman's conquest of the area in late 1863 opened the way for his massive invasion of Georgia.

Chattanooga also houses the locomotive *General* captured by federal troops in Georgia and raced back toward Tennessee as its captors destroyed bridges and railroad installations along the way in a daring raid that inspired the film *The Great Locomotive Chase*.

A later train episode – the 1900 wreck on the Illinois Central Line in Mississippi, piloted by a Tennessean named John Luther "Casey" Jones, led to a song bearing his name and a railroad museum in Jackson dedicated to his contribution to local folklore.

If people in Tennessee weren't singing about railroad disasters or Davy Crockett, they were singing about struggles and hardship in love and life in the cotton fields, on the great river – the Mississippi – or on Beale Street in Memphis, the first urban street and section in America where Negroes felt they were at home. Beale Street became home of the blues, and W.C. Handy, musician and composer, became father of the blues.

Tens of thousands of Negroes moved away from slavery and poverty all over the rural South after the war and passed through Memphis, often staying for a good while, on their way out to other battles and challenges of their own in the North. Many of them carried scars on their bodies and in their minds about the South and didn't ever want to be reminded of it.

But every time they heard some of those doggone blues coming up from Memphis, coming out of the black man's soul, they too felt a yearning for home back down South.

KENTUCKY

Kentucky, its name derived from an Indian word meaning "Land of Tomorrow," has as its state motto, "United We Stand, Divided We Fall." That feeling motivated it to stay within the Union during the Civil War, the only state included in this volume to do so. However, an estimated 45,000 Kentuckians fought with the Confederacy so that often brothers or father and son faced each other in battle. One Kentuckian, Abraham Lincoln, led the Union. Another, Jefferson Davis, headed the Confederacy. Even Lincoln's Kentucky-born brother-in-law fought with Confederate troops.

Ft. Harrod, built in 1774 (now reconstructed in Harrodsburg), helped protect early settlers from Indian attacks. Kentucky's first school was in the fort. And it was there that George Rogers Clark planned his expedition to free the Midwest from British control.

Earlier Kentuckians were united in their determination to open new lands and protect themselves against the Indians. Daniel Boone led a group of settlers through the Cumberland Gap and founded Boonesboro in 1775. Kentucky County was formed as a part of Virginia the next year but entered the Union in 1792 as a separate state.

Another community was settled at Bardstown in 1778 and today considers itself the "Bourbon capital of the world." Besides its unique Museum of Whisky History, one can see the mansion "Federal Hill," built in 1795 for U.S. Senator John Rowan, which inspired Stephen Foster to write the state song, "My Old Kentucky Home," "Wickland," an elegant Georgian mansion built in 1817, which became the birthplace of three governors, and St. Joseph's Cathedral, built in 1819, the oldest Catholic cathedral west of the Allegheny Mountains.

In 1805, members of The United Believers in Christ's Second Appearing – the Shakers – founded a colony near Fort Harrod at Pleasant Hill that prospered for nearly 50 years and produced some of the simplest yet most functional architecture and furniture design in the region. Another colorful group of settlers isolated themselves in the mountains and preserved until today, in their folksongs, Elizabethan ballads as they were sung by past generations of English descendants and which they still play on dulcimers.

Warring against Indians bred hawkish attitudes against other enemies as well in Kentucky. It was Congressman Henry Clay, one of the most powerful national politicians, who, with his fiery oratory, persuaded the young nation to declare war against England in 1812. Henry Clay's distinguished 20-room mansion, called "Ashland," can be seen in Lexington as can "Hopemont," the home of both John Wesley Hunt, the state's first millionaire, who built the house in 1814, and of John Hunt Morgan, a notorious Confederate raider.

Fighting also came naturally to the mountaineers of Kentucky, who became known for both their moonshine whisky and their family feuds, such as those between the Hatfields and the McCoys.

But no feud was as nasty as the Civil War. A shrine and diorama at Perryville, near the capital of Danville, marks the spot where, on October 8, 1862, 100,000 Union and Confederate troops locked in deadly combat. Within the few hours the battle lasted 6,000 soldiers lay dead on the field.

With the end of the conflict most Kentuckians decided to unite and put their minds to more pleasant things, such as raising and breeding thoroughbred horses in the lush blue-green meadowlands in the center of the state and racing and betting on them at Churchill Downs in Louisville, where the first Kentucky Derby was held in 1875. The wild excitement of Derby Week, accompanied by the drinking of a noble number of mint juleps, has become as important to Kentuckians as the frenzied, carnivalistic masquerading and dancing at Mardi Gras has become to New Orleans revelers. The truth is that Southerners have always loved a pageant, and the more colorful the better.

In spite of such diversions, initial efforts to industrialize the state with mining were painful to many Kentucky workers. A new form of economic exploitation made poor Appalachian miners no better off than plantation slaves and again made the state's ideal of unity among all its citizens a difficult one to attain for decades.

SOUTH CAROLINA

South Carolina was always a little hoity-toity, which was fine if you happened to be a landowner, or "lord proprietor."

William Sayle, an Englishman, created the first permanent settlement in South Carolina in 1670 on the Ashley River and called it Charles Towne in honor of King Charles II. Ten years later the community moved to its present site, keeping the name. Tenants and proprietors squabbled over rent collections and constitutional rights until the latter agreed to the creation of a more popular government in 1693.

As early as 1700, slaves were being sold to help with the cultivation of rice and by 1708 represented more than half of the colony's population. In 1712 two separate governors ruled over South and North Carolina until they were formally divided in 1815. Planters, many of whom were English and came from the already crowded island of Barbados, became wealthy from rice and indigo as traders did from selling deer skins. Meanwhile they had to fight off the Spanish (1686), the French (1706) pirates like Blackbeard and Indians (throughout the early 1700's) and the British in 1776. After capturing Charles Towne in 1780 the British moved inland but were defeated in several key battles (at King's Mountain and Cowpens) by backcountry leaders who thus ended British hopes of controlling the South.

Once the South Carolinians of means had time to devote to themselves they created some of the most beautiful architecture, which epitomized the charm and grace of the Old South. And around their lovely homes they planted gardens which are still landmarks. Middleton Place Gardens, begun in 1741, are the oldest landscaped gardens in the United States and have exhibits of life in both the 18th and 19th centuries worth seeing.

Charles Towne (renamed Charleston in 1783) became a commercial and cultural center – an aristocrat's cup of tea – and boasts of having staged the first opera performance, in about 1702 and of possessing one of the country's first museums in 1773. Musical societies like the St. Cecilia Society evolved into sponsors of debutante balls to present the most dazzling of Southern belles to society. And "The Southern Review," founded in 1823 in Charleston, fomented a rich literary production for which the South as a whole is known. Beaufort, Georgetown and Columbia also developed a richness of lifestyles and architecture.

Trade with Europe was essential to South Carolina, so the state opposed the first federal tariffs designed to protect northern manufacturers at its expense. It called a still higher tariff in 1828 the "Tariff of Abominations," and it declared an even higher tariff in 1832 null and void. A compromise on that issue in 1833 saved face for both sides.

When negotiations were no longer possible on the slavery question, John C. Calhoun led South Carolina to be the first state to secede from the Union. If South Carolina joined the Union of its own free will, he argued, it had the right to withdraw from it as well.

The famous first shot that started the Civil War was fired at Fort Sumter in Charleston. South Carolina's initiative cost it dearly, as 22 percent of its population died from the war that ensued. A Union blockade of Charleston Harbor and Sherman's devastating march north from Savannah to Columbia, which he burned, destroyed most of the state's economy.

After recovering from a particularly harsh Reconstruction rule, South Carolina moved slowly and painfully toward modernization, with the textile industry at the forefront. However, that development continued a clear-cut division of the haves (prosperous owners and managers) and the have-nots (the poor and often mistreated workers), with violence often used to keep workers in their place.

As both blacks and whites found out, the Old South, even as it was becoming "new," was a sad place to be poor. It would still take several generations after the great war before aristocratic privilege would be replaced by democratic fairness.

NORTH CAROLINA

North Carolina's state motto is "To Be, Rather Than To Seem," an appropriate saying for a people so unconcerned with pretense and appearances.

Just being was hard enough to accomplish in the early days. The first two English colonies on Roanoke Island, in 1585 and 1587, failed. Only in 1607 did their countrymen establish their first permanent settlement in Jamestown, Virginia. About 1,650 settlers trekked southward into the area of Albemarle Sound to establish their first home in North Carolina. In 1663 England's King Charles II carved up "Carolina" (including both North and South Carolina) and gave it to eight lord proprietors. In 1712 the colony was divided into North and South Carolina. By 1765 North Carolina was the fourth most populous of the 13 colonies, settled by English, Welsh, Germans, Highland Scots and Scotch Irish. Moravians founded the village of Salem in 1766, which has been restored near Winston-Salem, allowing a colorful look at the life of those early settlers.

From early times North Carolinians were a cantankerous bunch in defying English taxes and rule before the Revolutionary War. In 1774 patriots defied British authority by meeting in Tryon Palace, built by Royal Governor William Tryon (now restored in New Bern), to elect delegates to the First Continental Congress. North Carolina prides itself on being the first colony to instruct its delegates to the Continental Congress in 1776 to vote for independence. Then they dragged their heels in approving the U.S. Constitution because they opposed a strong federal government.

Until the 1830s North Carolina was a poor, backward state ruled by, and for the benefit of, a landed aristocracy. After that time the growing of cotton and tobacco prospered and was accompanied by light manufacturing, the exploration of gold as well as the construction of roads, railroads and schools in the western part of the state.

North Carolina refused to support South Carolina in its nullification of federal tariff laws in 1832 and was the last state to secede and join the Confederacy, as it did on May 20, 1861. Nevertheless, North Carolinians fought bravely for the South. Its blockade runners sailed in and out of Wilmington and managed to keep supplies coming to Confederate troops until almost the end of the war in 1865. Sometimes the locals fought harder than the Confederate Army. On one occasion they became so disgusted with Confederate soldiers who had retreated after one battle that they threatened to put tar on their heels the next time to make them stick around. Since then North Carolinians have been called "Tar Heels."

In spite of widespread destruction during the Civil War, the loss of 40,000 men and the freeing of 350,000 slaves,

North Carolina was fast to recover. Plantations were divided into smaller farms. Washington Duke established a smoking tobacco business at Durham in 1865. By 1880 there were 130 tobacco factories in the state. In 1890 Duke's son James Buchanan Duke started the American Tobacco Company.

About that time the state began to become a resort for the wealthy. George Vanderbilt of New York built his "Biltmore" estate in Asheville, one of the largest private homes in the world. Furniture making also helped diversify the state's economy so that it could take off into a new era of prosperity about the time the Wright Brothers made the first successful, powered airplane flight at Kitty Hawk.

Although very much into the new South now, North Carolina has been more respectful and protective of its rich Indian heritage than most other states in the nation. One need only see the performance "Unto These Hills" on the Cherokee Indian Reservation in the Smoky Mountains National Park or visit the Oconeluftee Indian Village nearby to see, appreciate and admire the really Old South.

VIRGINIA

Virginia, home of eight U.S. presidents, reeks of American history. Among other things, it can claim the first permanent English settlement, at Jamestown in 1607, the first planting of tobacco and the marriage of colonist John Rolfe in 1612 to Pocahontas, daughter of an Indian chief.

Already in 1619 Virginia was allowed to have its own representative legislature – the House of Burgesses – the first in America. Jamestown remained the capital until 1699, when it was moved to Williamsburg, the name of which was changed that year from Middle Plantation in honor of King William III (and the restoration of which today gives the best view anywhere of colonial life) and then to Richmond in 1779, two years before traitor Benedict Arnold led British troops to loot and burn the capital.

At first the thriving colony remained loyal to the British Crown, so much so that the aristocratic planters who settled in Virginia's Tidewater area clearly imitated the lifestyle of English country gentlemen. They had a sense of *noblesse oblige* which led many of them to assume positions of national leadership. But they made their money from land and slaves.

The passage of tax laws by Parliament in the 1760s and 1770s quickly strained the ties with England, and Virginia became a hotbed of advocacy for states' rights and later for independence. it was a Virginian, Patrick Henry, who on March 23, 1775 at Richmond's St. John's Church said, "Is life so dear or peace so sweet as to be purchased at the price of chains and slavery? Forbid it, Almighty God. I know not what courses others may take, but as for me give me liberty or give me death."

Another native, Thomas Jefferson, drafted the Declaration of Independence. Yet another, George Washington, led the Revolutionary forces that forced Britain's Lord Cornwallis to surrender at Yorktown, Virginia in 1781, and became the country's first president. Virginia also supplied the third, fourth and fifth presidents of the United States (as well as others later) and the chief justice of the Supreme Court, John Marshall (who served from 1801 to 1835).

Virginia gradually became more regionally oriented after the War of 1812, siding with the South on states' rights, including the right of secession, and slavery. John Brown's raid on Harpers Ferry in 1859, with the intention of causing a slave uprising, was a critical event in pitting slave holder against abolitionist, South against North.

Virginia didn't immediately follow its sister states in seceding but did so once President Abraham Lincoln called on it for troops to fight the South. A group of 48 counties in northwest Virginia maintained loyalty to the Union and seceded from Virginia, becoming the state of West Virginia in 1863.

Virginia had much of its territory ravaged by four years of battle, especially once the Confederacy moved its capital to Richmond in May, 1861.

Virginia did start up a few cigarette factories, shipyards and textile mills after the war, but it remained depressed until about World War I.

Thankfully, some of the best examples of early American architecture survived the war, such as "Monticello," the home of Thomas Jefferson, designed by him, as was the capitol building in Richmond and the Rotunda at the University of Virginia; the "Westover" plantation on the James River, built by William Byrd in the 1730s; and George Washington's stately residence "Mount Vernon" on the Potomac River.

In addition to being a testimonial to a golden age of architecture, Virginia is also a memorial to freedom, peace and unity. It's a place where truce ended war: the Revolutionary War in Yorktown, the Civil War at the Appomatox Court House. Its hills and valleys are littered with the graves of soldiers who fought in those wars.

May they and the quarrels that took them into combat rest in peace. And may the differences among peoples in various regions or nations be ones that distinguish them, not divide them.

These pages: Mount Vernon in Virginia, the beloved home of George Washington. (Top left) the Mansion. (Top right) interior of the Green House. (Left) exterior view of the office. (Above) the graveled driveway up to the Mansion. Facing page: the verandah behind the Mansion.

(Top left) the statue of Thomas Jonathan Jackson in Old Charlottesville, Virginia. (Top center) statue in memory of James Rogers McConnell, who was killed in battle whilst serving with the Volunteer Army of France on March 19, 1917. It is inscribed, "Soaring like an Eagle, into new Heavens of Valor and Devotion". (Left) the statue of Robert E. Lee in Lee Park. (Above) the James Monroe Statue.

(Far left) "Stonewall" Jackson's grave at Lexington Presbyterian Church. (Left) the Lee Statue on Monument Avenue, Richmond. (Bottom left) Washington Memorial Statue, Capitol Square. (Bottom center) "Stonewall" Jackson's statue and memorial on Monument Avenue. (Bottom right) Jefferson Davis Memorial and grave, Hollywood Cemetery. (Below) statue of J.E.B. Stuart.

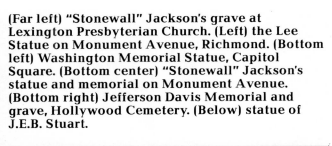

21

(Above) the fire house of the old U.S. Armory in Harper's Ferry, which John Brown, the abolitionist, used as the headquarters for his attack on the town in October 1859. Facing page: inside the dry goods store at Harper's Ferry. Overleaf: (left) New Market Battlefield Park. In 1864, the Confederate General John C. Breckenridge ordered the cadets from the Virginia Military Institute into active service. After marching the 90 miles from Lexington in three days, they were mistakenly placed in the front lines, where they fought heroically to help win the battle. (Right) Monticello, the beautiful home of Thomas Jefferson. Begun in 1769, this is regarded as a classic example of American architecture.

(Top left) on the Chatham Estate a "Union soldier" tends his campfire. (Top center) the regimental monument at Bloody Angle, part of the Fredericksburg and Spotsylvania National Military Park. (Above) on Marye's Heights is the Hugh Mercer Monument. (Far left) the statue and monument of Brigadier General Andrew Atkinson Humphries. (Left) the Thomas Jefferson Freedom Monument.

Facing page: (top left) a painting depicting the opening scene of the Battle for Fredericksburg. (Top right) the Richard Kirkland Monument. (Bottom right) one of the cannons of the Washington Artillery. (Bottom left) a plaque commemorating the Fredericksburg Campaign.

IN MEMORIAM
RICHARD ROWLAND KIRKLAND
CO. G, 2ND SOUTH CAROLINA VOLUNTEERS
C.S.A.

AT THE RISK OF HIS LIFE, THIS AMERICAN
SOLDIER OF SUBLIME COMPASSION BROUGHT
WATER TO HIS WOUNDED FOES AT
FREDERICKSBURG. THE FIGHTING MEN ON
BOTH SIDES OF THE LINE CALLED HIM
"THE ANGEL OF MARYE'S HEIGHTS."

FELIX DE WELDON
SC. 1965

FREDERICKSBURG CAMPAIGN

December 13, 1862. On this ridge, called Marye's
Heights, blazed the cannon of Col. J.B. Walton's Louisiana
battalion, the Washington Artillery. Late in the day,
out of ammunition, it yielded the post to Col. E. P.
Alexander's Reserve Artillery. Gen. Robert Ransom's North
Carolina infantrymen supported the guns and reinforced Cobb's Georgians
and Kershaw's South Carolinians in the Sunken Road below. The open field of
attack was raked "as with a fine-tooth comb," Alexander assured corps
commander James Longstreet. "A chicken could not live on that field."

United States Department of the Interior   National Park Service

Kenmore was the home of Betty Fielding Lewis, George Washington's sister. The house retains most of its original paneling and fine plasterwork. At the foot of the garden at Kenmore stands the house, a Dutch Colonial cottage, which Washington bought for Mary, his mother, in 1772.

These pages: Stratford Hall, in Westmoreland County, Virginia, exemplifies all the elegance of the 'Old Dominion' architectural style. Built between 1725 and 1730, Stratford was the birthplace of Francis Lee and Richard Henry Lee, the only brothers to sign the Declaration of Independence. It was also the birthplace of Robert E. Lee.

(Top left) the nursery.
(Above) the Great House.
(Far left) the dining rooms.

Facing page: (top left) the parlor. (Top right) the kitchen. (Bottom right) the Blue Bedroom, which was used as the guest room. (Bottom left) the wash house.

This page: Appomattox Court House National Historical Park, containing the site of General Robert E Lee's surrender of the army of Northern Virginia to General Ulysses S. Grant in 1865. (Top left) the guest house. (Top right) Isabell House. (Left) the Kelly House. (Above) Meeks store. Facing page: the parlor of the Presbyterian manse in Staunton, birthplace of President Thomas Woodrow Wilson.

This page: the mansion house on the Shirley Plantation, built between 1720 and 1740. The estate has been owned by the Carter family since the 17th century. Facing page: the mansion of the Westover Plantation was built in 1730-34 by William Byrd II, the founder of Richmond.

This page: the Berkeley Plantation, where the first official Thanksgiving service in America was held on December 4, 1619. During the Civil War it was the headquarters of General McClellan in the Seven Days' Battles. Facing page: the mansion at Sherwood Forest Plantation.

These pages: the Petersburg National Battlefield was the scene en months of war between the Union armies of the James and the Potomac, and the Confederate army under General Robert E. Lee and P.G.T. Beauregard. The right of the Confederate forces was eventually crushed at Five Forks, which led to the evacuation of Petersburg. The siege lasted from June 15, 1864, to April 2, 1865. Total troop losses amounted to some 70,000 men.

(Top left) "Union soldier" at the company desk of Battery No. 9. (Above) a Confederate cannon. (Far left) loading and firing the gun. (Left) inside the Sutler Store.

Facing page: (top left) cannon at Fort Morton. (Top right and bottom right) loading and firing the Confederate cannon. (Bottom left) gun detachment with the battle flag of the Washington Artillery.

These pages: Colonial Williamsburg contains many picturesque buildings, including (left) a working windmill. The preservation project was set up by Reverend W.A.R. Goodwin and John D. Rockefeller Jr. The Governor's Palace (top left), facing the Palace Green, is the most elegant of the buildings in Williamsburg, and is surrounded by ten acres of beautiful gardens. The original palace was completed in 1720, but tragedy struck in 1781 when it was destroyed by fire. Virginia's first two governors, Patrick Henry and Thomas Jefferson, lived here, as did seven British colonial governors. Overleaf left: Colonial Williamsburg, including, (top left) the guard house; (bottom left) Colonial Street; (bottom right) Duke of Gloucester Street. Overleaf right: The Governor's Palace.

These pages: Colonial Williamsburg. (Left) the general court room in the Capitol. (Bottom right) the council chamber. The Capitol is a reconstruction of the original 1705 building which was destroyed by fire in 1747. (Below) the Governor's Palace kitchen. (Bottom left) the Raleigh Tavern was the local political and social center, where figures such as Washington, Jefferson and Henry gathered.

These pages: six miles southeast of Colonial Williamsburg is the Georgian mansion of Carter's Grove, built between 1750 and 53. In the early 1700s, Robert "King" Carter, the richest of the Virginia planters, bought the 1,400 acres of land upon which his grandson, Carter Burwell, built the three-storey mansion house. Fine workmanship in loblolly-pine and walnut helps make this one of the most beautiful houses in America.

(Left) mansion house on Chippokes Plantation, Surry County. (Bottom left) Rolfe Warren House, also in Surry County. (Bottom right) a house on the Newmarket Battlefield. (Below) Chatham, Fredericksburg. Facing page: Prestwould Plantation, Clarkesville.

Winston-Salem, North Carolina, is a city with a wealth of houses which reflect its European heritage. Previous pages: (left) a weather-boarded shoemaker's shop, and (right) Elm House Tavern, which first opened its doors to travelers in 1784. (Above) the apothecary, and (facing page) the houses of Old Salem.

(Above) Linville Falls in the Pisgah National Forest, southern Appalachian Mountains, was named after William Linville, a contemporary of Daniel Boone killed by Indians nearby. Facing page: The Winkler Bakery, Winston-Salem North Carolina. Overleaf: Great Smoky Mountain National Park, (left) overlooking Maggie Valley.

Charleston, South Carolina, is a city with a unique heritage of stately houses and fine public buildings. (Above) the City Hall. Facing page: St. Michael's Episcopal Church in Broad Street. Overleaf: (left) the Dock Street Theatre, and (right) a beautiful setting for some of Charleston's historic buildings.

(Above) Joseph Manigault House in Charleston. Facing page: The National Russell House, Charleston, was constructed in 1809, and the interior is still decorated with exquisite furniture of the period.

Facing page: tranquil waters in the gardens of Middleton Place, South Carolina. Begun in
1741, these are the oldest landscaped gardens in America. This page and overleaf left:
nine original slave houses, lining the "Avenue of the Oaks", have been preserved on the
Boone Hall Plantation, South Carolina. In striking contrast is the splendor of beautiful
Drayton Hall, (overleaf right).

In Great Smoky Mountains National Park, Tennessee, mist
hangs between the tree covered mountain slopes (above), seen
from Newfound Gap Road. Facing page: overhung with trees,
Little Pigeon River rushes along its boulder-strewn bed.

For real peace of mind it would be hard to better the soothing effect of water as it tumbles and falls over rocks and weirs, or makes its hurried or placid way between tree-lined banks. Little River in the Smoky Mountains National Park (facing page) and (below) an old mill in Pigeon Forge, Tennessee.

The State Capitol in Nashville, Tennessee (these pages) is an outstanding example of Ionic Greek style architecture. Overleaf: (left) the lovely Belle Meade Mansion, built in 1853, was once the mansion house of a 5,300-acre plantation, well-known for the breeding of racehorses. (Right) the city of Memphis.

Riverboats line the banks at Memphis, Tennessee. Andrew Jackson, later President of the United States, helped to found the "Town of Memphis" in 1819. It was named after the ruined capital of ancient Egypt, on the banks of the Nile, because of its situation overlooking another great river; the Mississippi.

Within the Victorian Village area of Memphis are the Fontaine House of 1870 (top left) and (above) the James Lee House, built between 1848 and 1871. In Helena, Arkansas, can be found Major James Alexander Tappan House (left) and (facing page) the Short-Bieri House of 1901.

This page: to the south of Memphis is Chucalissa, a rebuilt Indian village which had disappeared between de Soto's visit in 1541 and the arrival of Joliet and Marquette in 1673. Facing page: mighty bridges span the Mississippi.

Previous pages: (right) Lapham-Patterson House, a restored, three-story Victorian mansion in Thomasville, South Georgia. (Left) the County Courthouse, Chatsworth, Georgia.

Reminders of the Civil War abound in Georgia, as at Kennesaw Mountain National Battlefield Park (far left, left and below center) and the Chickamauga Military Park (below, below far left and facing page), America's oldest and largest national military park.

WARREN'S MISSISSIPPI LIGHT ARTILLERY.
2 NAPOLEONS; 2 JAMES.
LIDDELL'S BRIGADE, LIDDELL'S DIVISION, WALKER'S CORPS.
SEPT. 20, 1863.
1ST LIEUT. H. SHANNON, COMMANDING,
2ND LIEUT. W. P. McDONALD MORTALLY WOUNDED.

THIS BATTERY WAS ALSO KNOWN AS SWETT'S BATTERY. WITH ITS BRIGADE IT MOVED
TO THE EXTREME RIGHT IN SUPPORT OF GEN. BRECKINRIDGE'S DIVISION IN THE MORNING
AND REMAINED IN POSITION WITHOUT BECOMING ENGAGED TILL THE AFTERNOON. ABOUT
5 P. M. THE BATTERY WAS ORDERED FORWARD BY THE REED'S BRIDGE ROAD COMING INTO
POSITION ON THIS GROUND ON THE RIGHT OF ITS DIVISION LINE. WHEN THE BATTERY OPENED
ON THE ENEMY ABOUT 800 YARDS NORTHWEST ARTILLERY FROM SEVERAL POINTS IMMEDIATELY
REPLIED COMPLETELY ENFILADING THE LINE OF INFANTRY. REYNOLDS DIVISION OF INFANTRY
IN PLAIN VIEW MOVING AT A DOUBLE-QUICK DIRECTLY AGAINST THE LEFT FLANK OF THE DIVISION
WITH THE ARTILLERY FIRE ABOVE MENTIONED MADE THE POSITION UNTENABLE. THE BATTERY
WAS ORDERED TO RETIRE WHICH IT DID AS RAPIDLY AS POSSIBLE LOSING ONE GUN BY THE LOSS
OF A HORSE WHICH WAS SOON AFTER RECOVERED BY THE ADVANCE OF CAPT. T. J. FLETCHER
AND A FEW MEN OF THE 13TH ARKANSAS. CASUALTIES OF THE BATTLE; KILLED 2 ENLISTED
MEN WOUNDED 1 OFFICER 8 ENLISTED MEN 11 HORSES KILLED OR DISABLED.

WARREN'S MISSISSIPPI LIGHT ARTILLERY.
2 NAPOLEONS; 2 JAMES.
LIDDELL'S BRIGADE, LIDDELL'S DIVISION, WALKER'S CORPS.
SEPT. 20, 1863.
1ST LIEUT. H. SHANNON, Commanding.
2ND LIEUT. W. P. McDONALD Mortally wounded.

THIS BATTERY WAS ALSO KNOWN AS SWETT'S BATTERY. WITH ITS BRIGADE IT MOVED
TO THE EXTREME RIGHT IN SUPPORT OF GEN. BRECKINRIDGE'S DIVISION IN THE MORNING
AND REMAINED IN POSITION WITHOUT BECOMING ENGAGED TILL THE AFTERNOON. ABOUT
5 P. M. THE BATTERY WAS ORDERED FORWARD BY THE REED'S BRIDGE ROAD COMING INTO
POSITION ON THIS GROUND ON THE RIGHT OF ITS DIVISION LINE. WITH THE BATTERY OPENED
ON THE ENEMY ABOUT 800 YARDS NORTHWEST ARTILLERY FROM SEVERAL POINTS IMMEDIATELY
REPLIED COMPLETELY ENFILADING THE LINE OF INFANTRY. REYNOLDS' DIVISION OF INFANTRY
IN PLAIN VIEW MOVING AT A DOUBLE-QUICK DIRECTLY AGAINST THE LEFT FLANK OF THE DIVISION
WITH THE ARTILLERY FIRE ABOVE MENTIONED MADE THE POSITION UNTENABLE. THE BATTERY
WAS ORDERED TO RETIRE WHICH IT DID AS RAPIDLY AS POSSIBLE LOSING ONE GUN BY THE LOSS
OF A HORSE WHICH WAS SOON AFTER RECOVERED BY THE ADVANCE OF CAPT. T. J. FLETCHER
AND A FEW MEN OF THE 13TH ARKANSAS. CASUALTIES OF THE BATTLE: KILLED 2 ENLISTED
MEN WOUNDED 1 OFFICER 8 ENLISTED MEN 11 HORSES KILLED OR DISABLED.

85

Atlanta's 25-acre Historical Society Complex contains carefully restored museum houses, amongst them Tullie Smith House (below) and Swan House (bottom left). (Bottom right) Governor's Mansion, Atlanta. (Left) Atlanta University. Facing page: an elegant Atlantan mansion set in beautiful gardens.

Georgia State University's gleaming white buildings are to be found in Athens (below and bottom pictures), as is Church Waddel Brumby House (facing page). (Left) Barrow County Court House in Winder, west of Athens.

MORGAN COUNTY

Morgan County was created by Act of Dec. 10, 1807 from Baldwin County. It was named for Gen. Daniel Morgan (1736-1802), a native of N. J. "Exactly fitted for the toils and pomp of war," he served with distinction on Benedict Arnold's expedition to Quebec in 1775-6, commanded the riflemen at Saratoga in 1777 and defeated Tarleton at Cowpens in 1781. After the War he served two terms in Congress. First county officers of Morgan County, commissioned January 14, 1808, were: Joseph White, Sh___; John Nesbitt, Clk. Sup. Ct.; Isham S. ___lk. Inf. Ct.; Daniel Sessions, Surveyor; ___oner.

GEORGIA HISTORICAL COMMISSION

"WE HERE HIGHLY RESOLVE THAT THESE DEAD SHALL
NOT HAVE DIED IN VAIN—THAT THIS NATION, UNDER
GOD, SHALL HAVE A NEW BIRTH OF FREEDOM—AND
THAT GOVERNMENT OF THE PEOPLE, BY THE PEOPLE,
FOR THE PEOPLE, SHALL NOT PERISH FROM THE EARTH."
(GETTYSBURG ADDRESS)
ABRAHAM LINCOLN.

ERECTED BY THE
STATE OF ILLINOIS
IN GRATEFUL REMEMBRANCE OF THE
PATRIOTIC DEVOTION OF HER SONS
WHO SUFFERED AND DIED IN THE
MILITARY PRISON AT ANDERSONVILLE, GA.
1864 — 1865

"THE 'MYSTIC CHORDS OF MEMORY, STRETCHING FROM
EVERY BATTLEFIELD AND PATRIOT GRAVE TO EVERY
LIVING HEART AND HEARTHSTONE ALL OVER THIS
BROAD LAND, WILL YET SWELL THE CHORUS OF THE
UNION, WHEN AGAIN TOUCHED, AS SURELY THEY WILL
BE, BY THE BETTER ANGELS OF OUR NATURE."
(FIRST INAUGURAL ADDRESS)
ABRAHAM LINCOLN.

Previous page, left: (top left) village near Madison, Georgia. (Remaining pictures) Morgan County Courthouse in Madison. Previous page, right: monument to the Civil War dead of Illinois in the Andersonville National Cemetery.

These pages and overleaf, left: the Victorian style houses of Augusta, Georgia. Overleaf, right: the white elegance of the coastal town of St. Mary's.

Americus flourished in the 1890s, and a number of Victorian-Gothic buildings remain (this page). Facing page: Stetson-Sanford House in the Georgia town of Milledgeville. Overleaf: (left) pillared Mercer University, and (right) Hay House, in Macon.

Westville, in Lumpkin (these pages), is a living history village which features pre-1850 buildings, and demonstrates the craft and decorative art skills of early Georgia.

HENRY SIMS MORGAN

2D LIEUTENANT
CORPS OF ENGINEERS
CLASS OF 1897
U. S. MILITARY ACADEMY

BORN OCTOBER 14, 1874
DROWNED AUGUST 31, 1899
WHILE ATTEMPTING TO RESCUE THE CREW
OF BARK NOE WRECKED IN TYBEE ROADS

ERECTED BY HIS CLASSMATES

113

Major restoration efforts have ensured that Savannah (these pages) is one of the most beautiful and historically rich cities in the South. The layout of its spacious squares and streets was conceived by General Oglethorpe, the city's founder.

Previous pages: views of Fort Pulaski in Savannah. The fort was named after Count Casimir Pulaski, who was killed here in battle against the British in 1779.

Savannah's houses (these and previous pages) exhibit a variety of architectural styles. (Facing page) Juliette Gordon Low's birthplace. Previous pages: (left) a Regency-style house, and (right) the bright stucco of the Pink House.

(Above) canoeing along the Suwannee River, which flows
gently through Florida from the Georgia line to the Gulf.

The Kingsley Plantation House (above), on Fort George Island, is believed to be the oldest plantation house in Florida, and has been restored as a house museum. Overleaf, left: a general store in Mobile, Alabama. (Right) Alabama's imposing State Capitol in Montgomery.

For eight years Mobile served as the capital of the French colonial empire, and today the elegance of this early French influence is reflected in its fine old mansions. Among the loveliest of these is Oakleigh (previous page, right and these pages), built between 1833 and 1838. Previous page, left, and overleaf: Gaineswood, Demopolis, one of the finest Greek Revival structures in the South.

Cotton has always been a major crop in Mississippi, as seen
(these pages) in Coahoma County. Today, modern machines
(opposite page) have taken the back-breaking hardship out
of its harvesting. (Above) a farmhand's cottage stands
flanked by the fields in which he works.

Moon Lake (these pages) lies to the north of Friars Point in Coahoma County, Mississippi. Subtle shades of pink and peach color the sky and the lake's surface from dawn (left), to bright day (top) and dusk (remaining pictures).

This page: bridges over the Mississippi River at Vicksburg and the 7.44-inch cannon nicknamed "The Widow Blakeley", which engaged gunboats on May 22, 1863. Facing page: (top left) Levee Street Station. (Top right and bottom left) the Shirley House. (Bottom right) Cedar Grove.

These pages: Vicksburg National Military Park, scene of the 47-day siege. President Abraham Lincoln had said, "Vicksburg is the key... The war can never be brought to a close until that key is in our pocket." He knew that without control of the city he would never control the Mississippi, and had told General Grant, "...the opening of the Mississippi River will be to us of more advantage than the capture of 40 Richmonds." A Confederate chaplain at the ensuing siege wrote of "men lying in ditches... under continual fire and on quarter rations... their strength is frittered away."

EUGENE ERWIN
COL. 6 TH MO. C. S. INFTY
KILLED IN BATTLE JUNE 25 1863

MISSISSIPPI

MISSISSIPPI

ILLINOIS

139

(Left) plaque on the Grand Gulf Historic tour. (Far left) an old cotton mill near Chatham. (Below) a derelict church at Grand Gulf. (Bottom left) a U.S. Army wagon of c1900 in the museum in the Grand Gulf Military Monument Park and (facing page, top left) the Water Mill. Facing page: (top right) Stanton Hall, Natchez, Mississippi. Near Port Gibson are the ruins of Windsor (bottom left), which burnt down in 1890. (Bottom right) Auburn, at Duncan Park, Natchez, was built in 1812 by Levi Weeks.

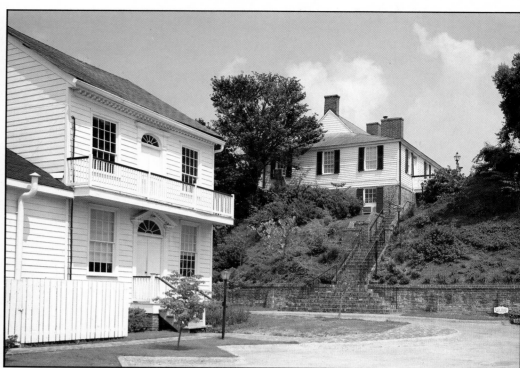

These pages: the stately architecture of Natchez, a reminder of days now past. (Top left) historic King's Tavern of 1789. (Above) Connelly's Tavern, built in 1795, on Ellicott Hill. (Top right) Priest's House. (Right) Rosalie, 1820, was the Federal headquarters during the occupation of Natchez. Facing page: beautiful Glen Auburn.

These pages: elegant Natchez facades: (top left) on Pleasant Hill; (above) along Union Street and (right) Commerce Street. (Top right) magnificent Rosalie. Facing page: Longwood, 1858-1861, was never completed as intended by its owner, Dr. Haller Nutt, but is now a National Historic Landmark.

146

Previous pages: (left) a stately house in the coastal town of Biloxi, Mississippi. (Right) the ornate splendor of the drawing room in Stanton Hall, built during the great cotton era using materials and furnishings from Europe. (Above) golden light on Lake Dardanelle in Russellville, Arkansas. Facing page: the Arkansas State Capitol.

Previous pages: dignified interior of the Old State House in Little Rock, Arkansas. Begun in 1833, this served as the state capitol from 1836 to 1911. (Above) the present State Capitol building, Little Rock. To the north lies Buffalo River State Park (facing page). Overleaf: (left) the Arkansas River flows through Little Rock. (Right) evening light on the State Capitol, Little Rock.

This page: many of the palatial homes built by the rich owners of Louisiana sugar and cotton plantations are now museums or hotels (top left). Facing page: the Old State Capitol in Baton Rouge, Louisiana, was built in 1847. Burnt down by a Federal army during the Civil War, it was repaired, and served as the State House until 1932.

These pages: the Myrtles, a well-restored plantation house in St. Francisville, Louisiana. The house was built circa 1796, and has a 110-foot gallery with iron grillwork, elaborate interior plasterwork, and beautifully landscaped grounds.

(Top left) the Pino House and (left) the Stewart-Dougherty House, Baton Rouge. (Above and facing page) Oakley House, St. Francisville, is the centerpiece of Audubon Memorial State Park. The plantation home has been furnished as it was in 1821 when John James Audubon (1785-1851), the artist and naturalist, lived here as tutor to the owner's daughter. During this time he painted 32 of the pictures which appeared in his monumental work, *The Birds of America*, which contained 435 hand-colored plates in 4 volumes.

These pages: the Rural Life Museum on the Burden Research Plantation of Louisiana State University. The Museum is a replica of a typical sugar plantation in the Mississippi Valley. Among the authentic buildings reconstructed on the site are an old schoolhouse, a general store, a blacksmith's workshop and an overseer's cottage. Within a large barn can be seen articles relating to traditional rural crafts and skills.

The University itself was originally established near Alexandria in 1860 and moved to Baton Rouge in 1869. Other museums at the LSU include the Anglo-American Museum in the Memorial Tower, the Geoscience Museum in the Geology Building and the Museum of Natural Science in Foster Hall. The Library contains a collection of the "elephant folio" paintings by Audubon and on the 200-acre campus, which contains some charming lakeside areas, are several Indian earthworks dating back over 750 years.

Plantation homes of the South: (top left) Nottaway Plantation; (left) Oak Alley Plantation, Vacherie; (above and facing page) Rosedown Plantation in St. Francisville. (Top) Houmas House at Burnside.

The first settlers came to New Orleans in search of furs, and found them in plenty. However, for Louisiana to grow rich a cash crop was needed. Both indigo and tobacco were tried, but it was not until the sugar plantations were established that the state really began to prosper. In 1795 the Louisianians perfected a process for granulating sugar, and the industry boomed. The owners of huge plantations which now grew up all over Louisiana spent some of their new-found wealth on magnificent town houses in New Orleans. Many of the mansions they built for themselves can still be seen along St. Charles Avenue (these pages).

Two faces of New Orleans (these pages). The elegant interior of a Creole mansion, Grimma House (this page), epitomises the grace and splendor of the Creole culture. Facing page: jazz, which reached an early high among the free Negroes of New Orleans, is still a way of life in the half-light of the city's bars and nightclubs.

71

Previous pages and overleaf left: delicate wrought-ironwork on the balconies of
old houses in the Vieux Carré, New Orleans. These pages: plantation owners often
turned to antiquity for inspiration when building their mansions. Columns
feature strongly in such houses, supporting balconies and porticoes, as in the
graceful Corinthian Mansion (facing page). Overleaf right: the Vieux Carré can
be seen in a leisurely fashion from a brightly painted, horse-drawn carriage.

INDEX